Historic and Lively
What Am I?

by Joyce Markovics

Consultant: Eric Darton, Adjunct Faculty
New York University Urban Design and Architecture Studies Program
New York, New York

New York, New York

Credits

Cover, © Matt McClain/Shutterstock; 2, © YAY Media AS/Alamy; TOC, © D. Hurst/Alamy; 4–5, © Frank Tozier/Alamy; 6–7, © RGB Ventures/SuperStock/Alamy; 8–9, © YAY Media AS/Alamy; 10–11, © David Stuckel/Alamy; 12–13, © Michele and Tom Grimm/Alamy; 14–15, © M. Timothy O'Keefe/Alamy; 16–17, © Jan Butchofsky/Alamy; 18–19, © David M. Doody/Colonial Williamsburg; 20–21, © David M. Doody/Colonial Williamsburg; 22, © Cephas Picture Library/Alamy; 23, © Mark Summerfield/Alamy; 24, © Bernd W. Herrmann/Shutterstock.

Publisher: Kenn Goin
Senior Editor: Joyce Tavolacci
Creative Director: Spencer Brinker
Design: Debrah Kaiser
Photo Researcher: Thomas Persano

Library of Congress Cataloging-in-Publication Data

Names: Markovics, Joyce, author.
Title: Historic and lively : what am I? / by Joyce Markovics.
Description: New York, New York : Bearport Publishing Company, 2018. | Series: American Place Puzzlers series | Includes bibliographical references and index.
Identifiers: LCCN 2017042963 (print) | LCCN 2017044612 (ebook) | ISBN 9781684025404 (ebook) | ISBN 9781684024827 (library)
Subjects: LCSH: Colonial Williamsburg (Williamsburg, Va.)—Juvenile literature. | Williamsburg (Va.)—Juvenile literature.
Classification: LCC F234.W7 (ebook) | LCC F234.W7 M37 2018 (print) | DDC 975.5/4252—dc23
LC record available at https://lccn.loc.gov/2017042963

Copyright © 2018 Bearport Publishing Company, Inc. All rights reserved. No part of this publication may be reproduced in whole or in part, stored in any retrieval system, or transmitted in any form or by any means, electronic, mechanical, photocopying, recording, or otherwise, without written permission from the publisher.

For more information, write to Bearport Publishing Company, Inc., 45 West 21st Street, Suite 3B, New York, New York 10010. Printed in the United States of America.

10 9 8 7 6 5 4 3 2 1

Contents

What Am I? 4
Fast Facts 22
Where Am I? 23
Index 24
Read More 24
Learn More Online 24
About the Author 24

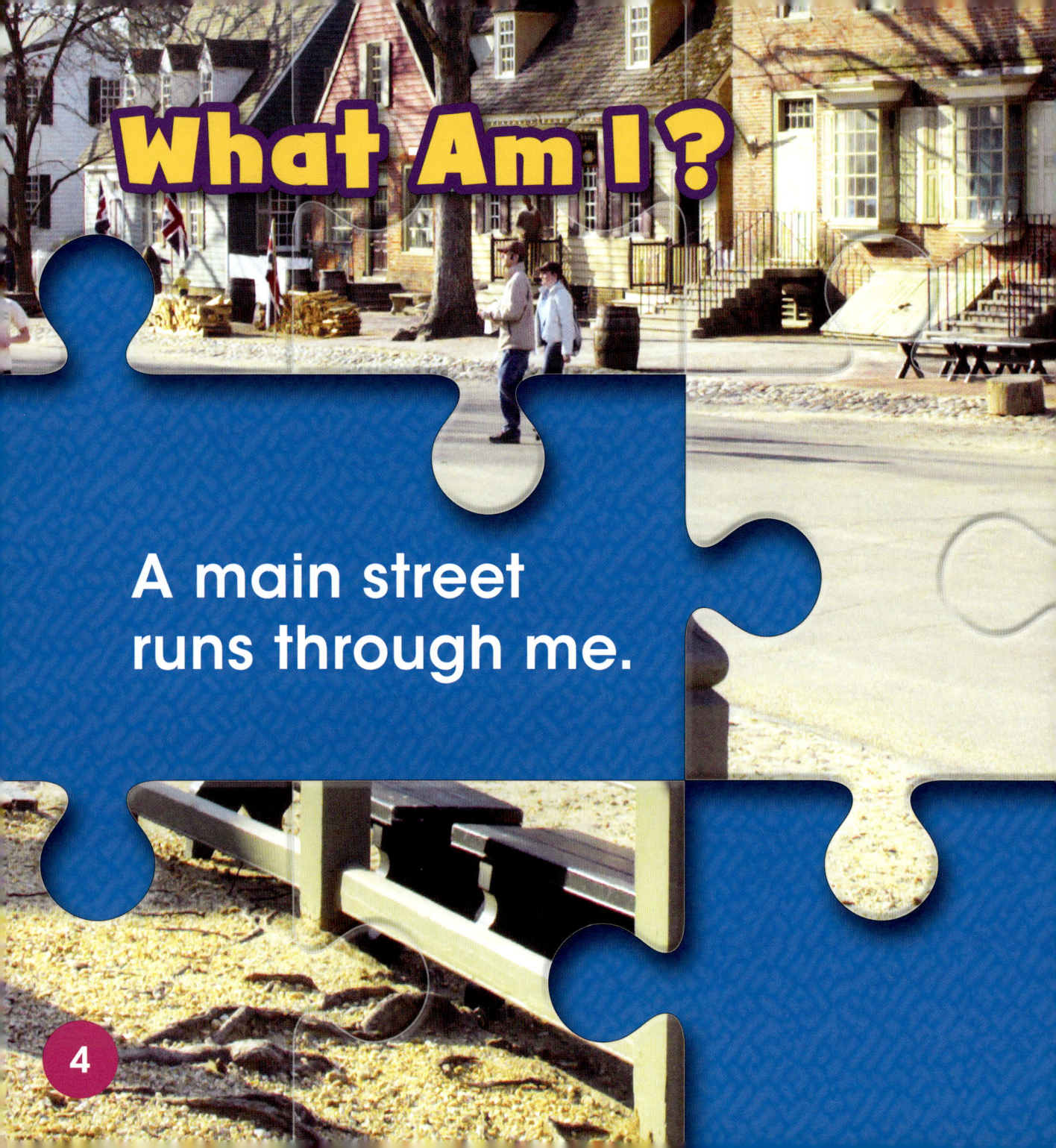

What Am I?

A main street runs through me.

I am home to beautiful gardens.

I have many historic buildings.

8

One was home to Virginia's governors.

9

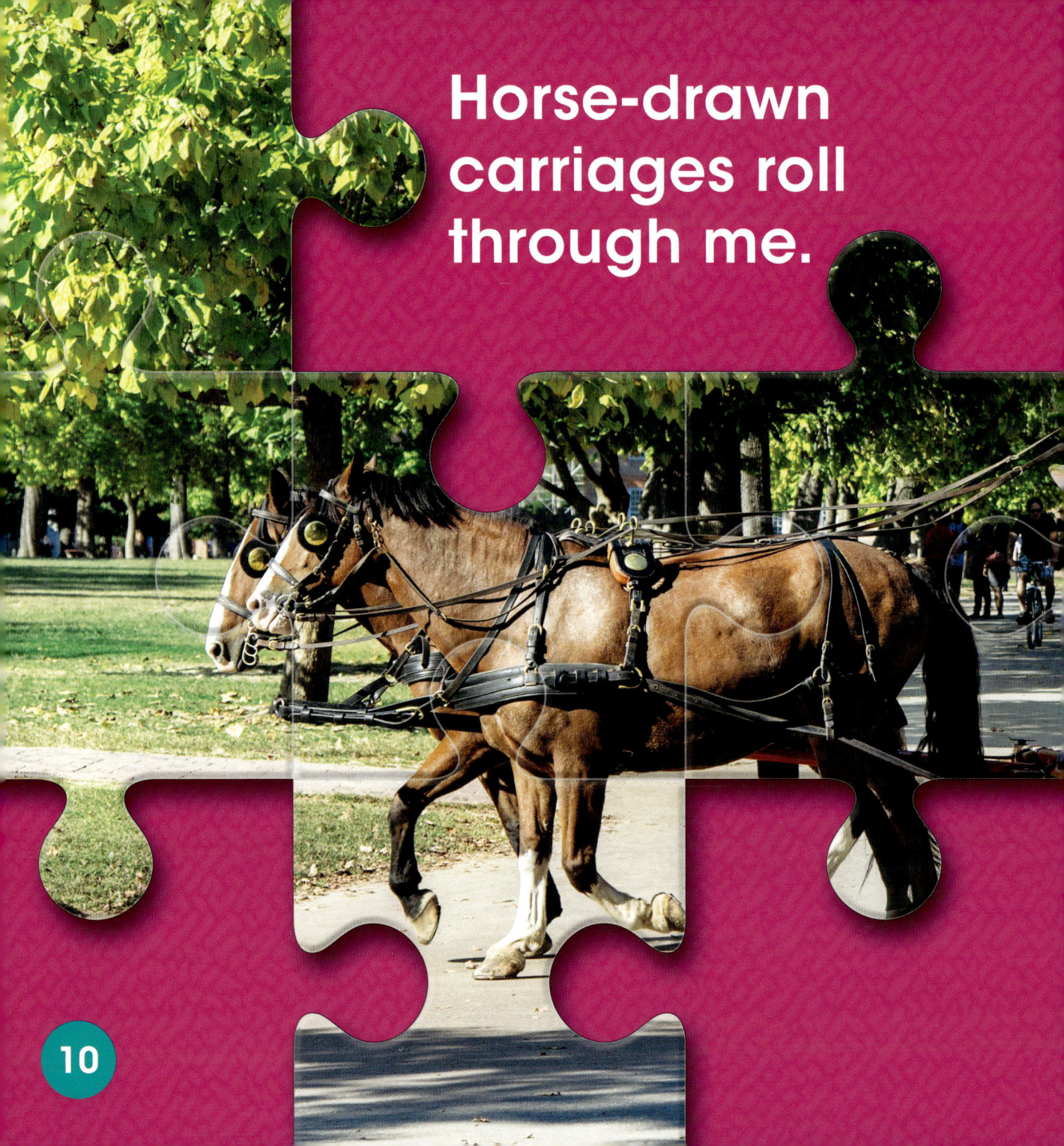

Horse-drawn carriages roll through me.

I have many workers.

They dress up like people who lived long ago.

13

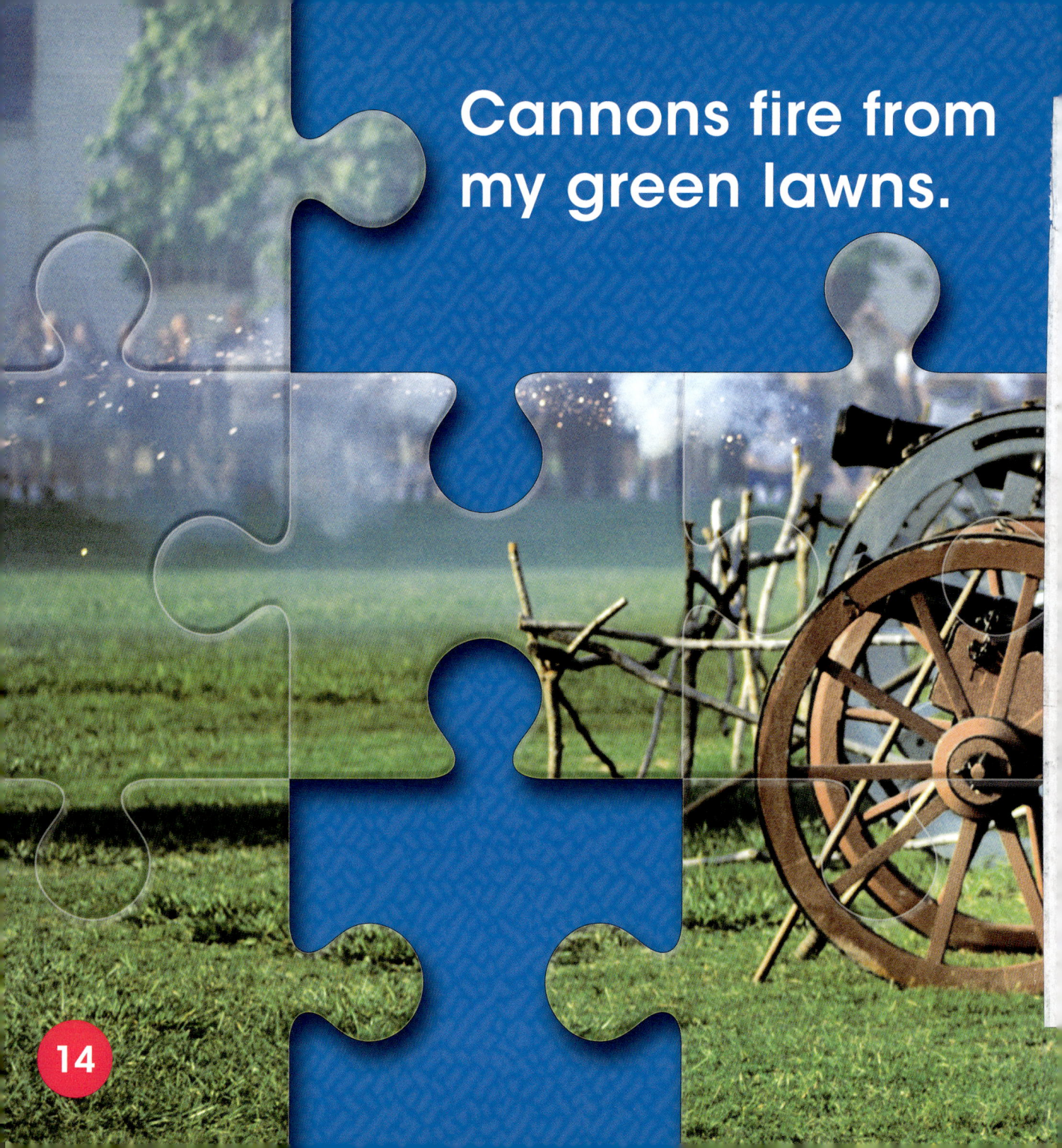

Cannons fire from my green lawns.

14

15

People from all over America visit me!

What am I?

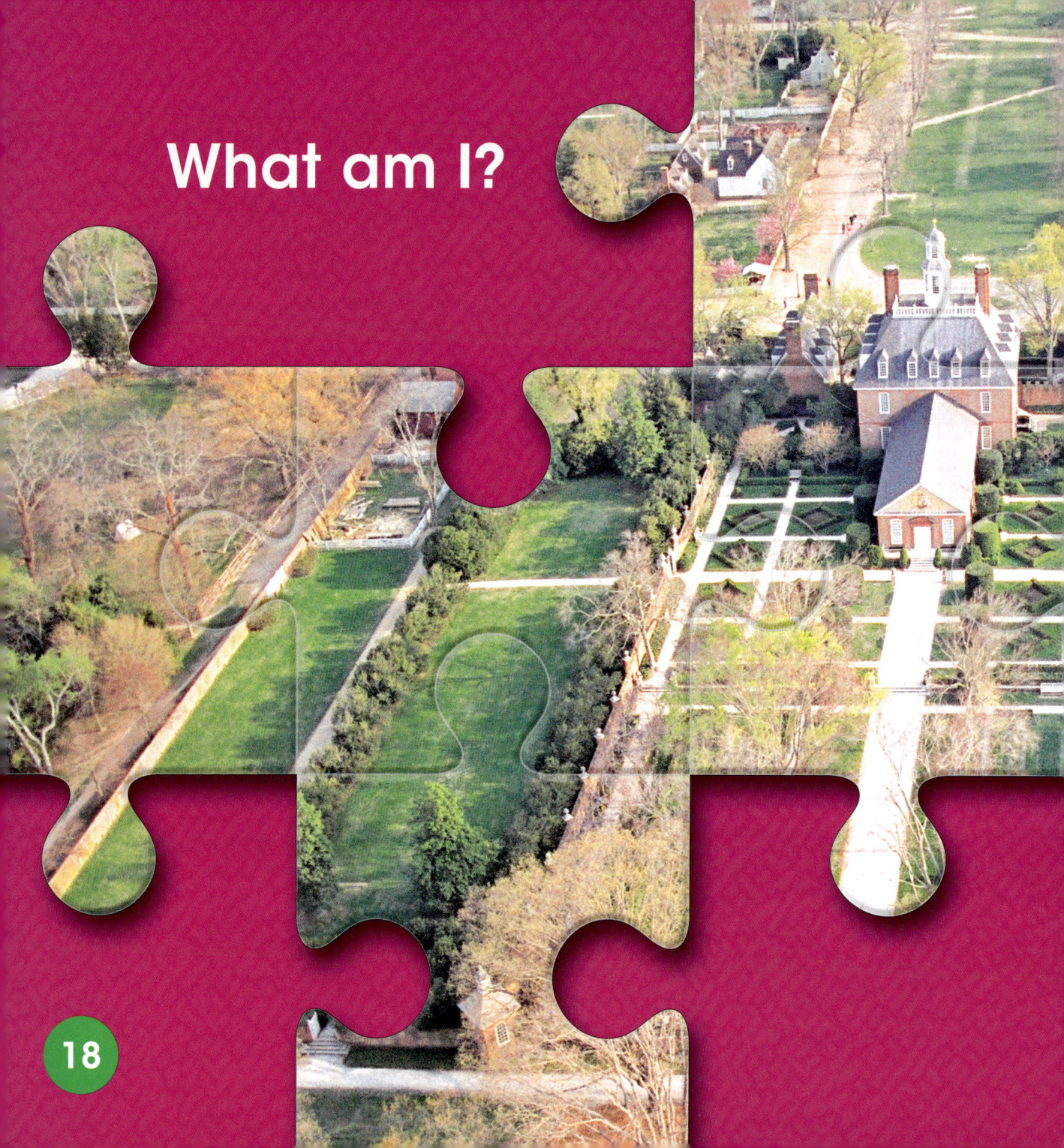

18

Let's find out!

19

Fast Facts

Colonial Williamsburg is a 301-acre (122 ha) historic area. It includes many buildings, some of which date to the 1600s and 1700s! Visitors travel to Colonial Williamsburg to see how people lived hundreds of years ago.

Colonial Williamsburg

Year the Town Was First Settled:	1632
Number of Historic Buildings:	88
Total Number of Buildings:	More than 500
Number of Years Williamsburg Served as Virginia's Capital:	81
Cool Fact:	Since Colonial Williamsburg opened in 1932, more than 100 million people have visited this historic site.

Where Am I?

Colonial Williamsburg is located in Williamsburg, Virginia.

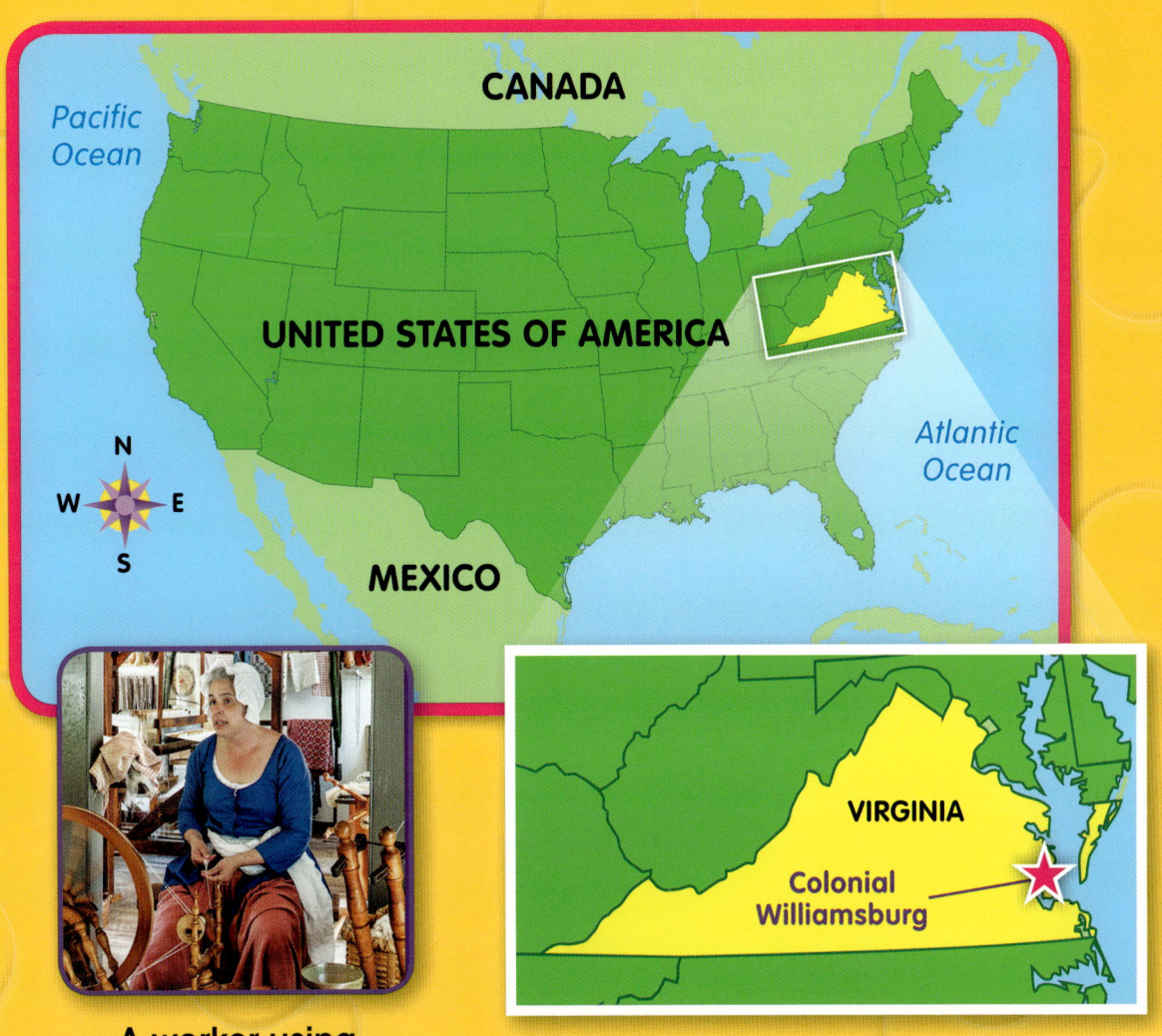

A worker using a spinning wheel

Index

buildings 8–9, 22
cannons 14–15
carriages 10–11
gardens 6–7
main street 4–5
Virginia 9, 22–23
visitors 16–17, 22
workers 12–13, 23

Read More

Brenner, Barbara. *If You Lived in Williamsburg in Colonial Days.* New York: Scholastic (2000).

Chorao, Kay. *D is for Drums: A Colonial Williamsburg ABC.* New York: Harry N. Abrams (2004).

Learn More Online

To learn more about Colonial Williamsburg, visit
www.bearportpublishing.com/AmericanPlacePuzzlers

About the Author

Joyce Markovics lives in an old house along the Hudson River. It was built around 1850—that's more than 150 years after the oldest structure in Colonial Williamsburg was built!